D0383123

John Paul Jones

The Continental Congress began to build a navy in 1775. The first naval battle was on January 5, 1776, with Commander-in-Chief Hopkins capturing gunpowder and cannons in the Bahamas.

The most famous naval hero in the Revolutionary War was John Paul Jones, who took his sailors all the way to England on a raid. First he hit the town of Whitehaven. Then he tried to attack Edinburgh but couldn't because of bad weather. Next, he burned some ships in the Humber River.

The battle with the *Serapis* and *Countess of Scarborough* took place on September 23, 1779, off Flamborough Head, on the eastern side of England.

Jones' exploit made him famous and greatly lifted the morale of the Americans.

Note: In the story, when the *Serapis* Captain asks, "Has your ship struck?" He is asking, "Do you surrender?"

Library of Congress Cataloging in Publication Data

Charles, Carole, 1943-
    John Paul Jones—Victory at Sea

    (Stories of the Revolution)
    SUMMARY: Relates in verse the battle between John Paul Jones' Bonhomme Richard and the British ships Serapis and Scarborough.
    1. Jones, John Paul, 1747-1792—Juvenile poetry.
2. United States—History—Revolution, 1775-1783
—Naval operations—Juvenile poetry. [1. Jones, John Paul, 1747-1792—Poetry. 2. United States—History—Revolution, 1775-1783—Naval operations—Poetry] I. Seible, Bob. II. Title.
PZ8.3.C383Jo   811'.5'4   75-33157
ISBN 0-913778-21-4

© 1975, The Child's World, Inc. All rights reserved.
Printed in U.S.A. Art and copy provided by TRIMEDIA.

Distributed by Childrens Press, 1224 West Van Buren Street, Chicago, Illinois 60607

John Paul Jones-
Victory at Sea

A Narrative Poem
by Carole Charles
pictures by Bob Seible

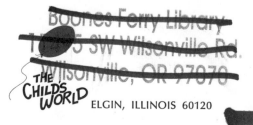

Boones Ferry Library
T_____5 SW Wilsonville Rd.
Wilsonville, OR 97070

THE CHILD'S WORLD ELGIN, ILLINOIS 60120

WEST LINN SCHOOL DISTRICT #31

John Paul Jones: There lie the ships! They'll be ours
tonight!
The British navy will see how we
fight!
Raise the flags to call our fleet!
Signal all four ships to meet!

The *Serapis* will fall into the hand
Of John Paul Jones, with his American
command.
The escort *Scarborough* will next be won,
Leaving the supply ships with hardly a gun.

The British navy needs those supplies,
But it's our good fortune to capture the prize.
If we stop their ships from crossing the sea,
America might win this war and be free.

Lieutenant! Why don't our ships come about?
The Cowards! They're letting me fight this one
    out!
Haul up the courses, prepare to fire!
The *Bonhomme Richard* will not retire!

The *Serapis* cuts through the water with ease,
Faster than our old ship 'fore the breeze.
She has more guns—she's strong all right.
We'll have to outsmart her to win this fight.

Fire broadside! These hits we can't afford!
We must close in and try to board.
No! We're too far back, I say!
That's not it! Pull away! Pull away!

The *Serapis* is coming around—Now!
Ram her stern with *Richard's* bow!
Serapis Captain: Has your ship struck? Do you give
up the fight?

John Paul Jones: I HAVE NOT YET BEGUN TO FIGHT!

We've fresh wind in our sails, pull out!
Bring the *Richard* full about.

That's it, men, right on her bow.
We'll board this British vessel now.

Aha! We're clapped together fast.
Lieutenant, there's fire on the mast!
Gunners, shoot every man on top,
We have to make those big guns stop.

Sailor: Sir, one of our ships fights the
Scarborough, there!
And here comes another of ours.
Sir! Beware!
John Paul Jones: She fires at us! What's she trying to
do?
Their captain will lose his command
when I'm through!

Again! Three times! He's out of his head!
Their captain wants glory, no matter who's dead!

Sailor: Captain, we've five feet of water below!

John Paul Jones: Man the pumps!

Sailor: Should we strike?

Jones: No, no, no, no!

Keep shooting! Keep pumping! Put out the
flame!
The *Serapis* still fires, give 'er back the same!
Aim at the mainmast! Sailors, take heart!

Sailor: But, Captain, our ship—it's all coming apart!

John Paul Jones: I'll defend *Bonhomme Richard* with
my last breath.
The mast of *Serapis*—it shivers with
death!
Their captain has struck! He gives
up the fight!
The *Serapis* is ours this September
night.

The *Serapis*, the *Scarborough*—two prizes this
    night;
But the British supply ships have sailed out of
    sight.
The *Richard* will sink; transfer the crew.
She's nothing but holes and a post or two.

Sailor: Captain Paul Jones, I'm amazed that
we won.
The British were stronger, gun for
gun.

John Paul Jones: But stronger than guns is my wish to
be free.
We held out—and won our battle at
sea.

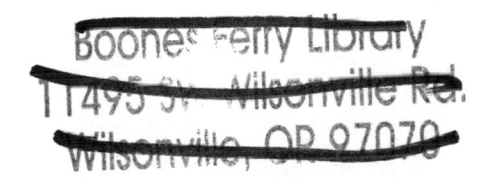

Boones Ferry Library
11495 SW Wilsonville Rd.
Wilsonville, OR 97070